PORTSMOUTH PUBLIC LIBRARY
175 PARROT AVENUE
PORTSMOUTH, NH 03801-4452
603-427-1540

WITHDRAWN
from
Portsmouth Public Library

FEB 07 2019

D1266991

UNCOVERING THE PAST:
ANALYZING PRIMARY SOURCES

GOLD RUSHES

NATALIE HYDE

CRABTREE
PUBLISHING COMPANY
WWW.CRABTREEBOOKS.COM

Author: Natalie Hyde

Editor-in-Chief: Lionel Bender

Editors: Simon Adams, Ellen Rodger

Proofreaders: Laura Booth, Angela Kaelberer

Design and photo research: Ben White

Production: Kim Richardson

**Production coordinator and
  prepress technician:** Ken Wright

Print coordinator: Katherine Berti

Consultants: Amie Wright, Emily Drew
  The New York Public Library

Produced for Crabtree Publishing Company
by Bender Richardson White

Photographs and reproductions:
Alamy: 8–9 (Chronicle), 13 (Andrew Fare); Getty Images: 18 (Bettmann),
19 (Corbis Documentary), 23 (Stefano Bianchetti), 24 (Archive Photos), 31
(Hulton Archive), 40–41 (Corbis Historical); Library of Congress: 1 (LC-DIG-
ppmsc-02669), 3 (LC-USZ6-511), Top Left (Icon) 4, 6, 8 (LC-USZ62-57280), 5
(LC-DIG-ppmsca-34503), 6 (LC-DIG-ppmsc-02029), 9 (LC-USZ62-50909), Top
Left (Icon) 10, 12, 14 (LC-USZ62-57280), Top Left (Icon) 16, 18 (LC-USZ6-511),
Top Left (Icon) 20, 22, 24, 26, 28, 30, 32 (LC-DIG-pga-08765), 20–21 (LC-DIG-
pga-01872), 28–29 (LC-DIG-pga-01999), 32 Left (LC-USZ62-57312), Top Left
(Icon) 34, 36 (LC-DIG-highsm-23829), 34–35 (LC-DIG-ppmsca-28732), 35
(LC-USZC4-11401), 36 (LC-USZ62-8544); Private Archive 11 top, 11 Btm;
Shutterstock: 12 (Emma Jones), 38, 40 Top Left (Icon) (Arsel Ozgurdal), 41
(Kubasiak Zbigniew); 4–5,Topfoto: 7, 16–17, 22, 26, 29, 30, 37 Top, (The Granger
Collection), 25, (Topfoto), 38–39, (Ullsteinbild); wikimedia.org: front cover (L.
C. McClure), 14, 37

Map: Stefan Chabluk

Cover:
Background: Miners coat of Arms.
Foreground: A Forty-niner peers into the silt on California's American River.

Library and Archives Canada Cataloguing in Publication

Hyde, Natalie, 1963-, author
    Gold rushes / Natalie Hyde.

(Uncovering the past: analyzing primary sources)
Includes bibliographical references and index.
Issued in print and electronic formats.
ISBN 978-0-7787-4748-2 (hardcover).--
ISBN 978-0-7787-4816-8 (softcover).--
ISBN 978-1-4271-2086-1 (HTML)

    1. Gold mines and mining--History--Juvenile literature.
2. Gold mines and mining--History--Sources--Juvenile literature.
I. Title.

TN420.H93 2018   j338.2'74109   C2017-907709-0
                                          C2017-907710-4

Library of Congress Cataloging-in-Publication Data

CIP available at the Library of Congress

Crabtree Publishing Company

www.crabtreebooks.com   1-800-387-7650

Printed in the U.S.A./022018/CG20171220

Copyright © **2018 CRABTREE PUBLISHING COMPANY**. All rights reserved. No part of this publication may be reproduced,
stored in a retrieval system, or be transmitted in any form or by any means, electronic, mechanical, photocopying, recording,
or otherwise, without the prior written permission of Crabtree Publishing Company. In Canada: We acknowledge the financial
support of the Government of Canada through the Canada Book Fund for our publishing activities.

Published in Canada
Crabtree Publishing
616 Welland Ave.
St. Catharines, ON
L2M 5V6

Published in the United States
Crabtree Publishing
PMB 59051
350 Fifth Avenue, 59th Floor
New York, NY 10118

Published in the United Kingdom
Crabtree Publishing
Maritime House
Basin Road North, Hove
BN41 1WR

Published in Australia
Crabtree Publishing
3 Charles Street
Coburg North
VIC, 3058

UNCOVERING THE PAST

THE PAST COMES ALIVE

"Universal history is... not a burden on the memory but an illumination of the soul."

Lord John Dalberg-Acton, historian and politician, 1895

The past is full of tales of adventure, success, failure, tragedy, comedy, and excitement. These are stories of what people achieved or lost in life. Looking back at the past gives us a chance to see how our ideas and values have shaped our world. Learning from our mistakes and repeating our successes are just two ways we can use the information of the past to help us prepare for the future.

Major events, such as the gold rushes in North America, affect many parts of **society**. The Klondike and California gold rushes of the 1800s changed history, geography, and the course of **immigration** and **settlement**. The use of foreign workers changed the cultural makeup of the West Coast. New laws were created to deal with what would happen to these workers when the mines closed. The need to move goods and supplies led to the building of new highways and railroads. New technologies were created to make mining faster and more productive.

This new wealth changed not only individuals, but also entire regions. Mines in **remote** areas opened up new sites for settlement. The settlements often **encroached** on **Indigenous peoples'** traditional lands. The miners brought new diseases to these people. They also changed the landscape by damming rivers and blasting through mountains. The North American gold rushes of the past brought changes we can see and study today.

▶ Columbia, California, was a boomtown thanks to the gold rush of 1848. By 1850 it had many hotels, banks, stores, churches, and **saloons**.

► During the earlier gold rushes, mining was hard, manual labor using simple tools like shovels and pickaxes.

EVIDENCE RECORD CARD

The California Gold Rush

LEVEL Primary source
MATERIAL Lithograph
LOCATION Columbia, California
DATE 1852
SOURCE Topfoto/Granger

DEFINITIONS

Boomtown: a settlement that grows rapidly from a camp to a thriving town
Forty-niner: a prospector who arrived for the California Gold Rush in 1849
Gold rush: people rushing to a newly discovered goldfield
Lode gold: gold found between layers of rock
Mining claim: land where a miner has the right to mine minerals from the ground
Pay streak: a layer of minerals
Placer gold: gold deposited near the surface of the ground
Prospector: an explorer of mineral deposits
Sluice box: a long, sloping box with grooves on the bottom to catch gold

INTRODUCTION

SOURCES OF EVIDENCE

Looking back at the gold rushes can raise a lot of questions. What happened there? Who took part? What was it like? Did miners strike lucky or fail?

We can find the answers to these questions by looking back at historical **evidence**. The **documents** and images, as well as stories and interviews, created at the time can give us that information. The amount of evidence that remains of any event depends on many factors. Natural disasters, such as floods, storms, and fires, can destroy any material in their path. The destruction from battles and civil wars also cause much evidence to be lost. Some evidence might survive but is kept hidden. This is true of information that might make a modern organization, such as a bank or a government, or an individual look bad.

Some evidence is carefully **preserved**. This is true of important historical people or events such as the moon landing. Sometimes evidence is preserved by accident. Old bronze church bells have been used as doorstops and parts of bombs used as paperweights. Dishes stored in an attic might have been wrapped with old newspapers that contain information on the Stock Market Crash of 1929 or on the moon landing in 1969.

There is a lot of evidence left from the gold rushes in North America. Cameras had been invented so we can study photographs of the mines and miners. There was **telegraphy,** too, so we can read telegrams and newspaper reports of mining activity. Mining required permits, licenses, land deeds, and claim records, making an additional **paper trail**. Among the thousands of people who took part are many who kept diaries or

▲ Gold is heavier than soil and rocks. In a sluice box, water washes the dirt away while the gold sinks to the bottom and can be collected easily.

"I cannot advise any person to come. But if any of our neighbours are determined to come, say them, to fix no time when they will return, and so arrange their business, that they may stay several years, for it will take more time to make a fortune than many have supposed."

Letter from prospector John Walker to his parents, December 24, 1850 journals of their adventures. And, as many men left wives and families behind, we can read many old letters that told of the highs and lows of life during that time.

Historians are experts on one time period, person, or event. Because the hunts for life-changing wealth in the gold rushes affected so many parts of society, there are many historians on the subject.

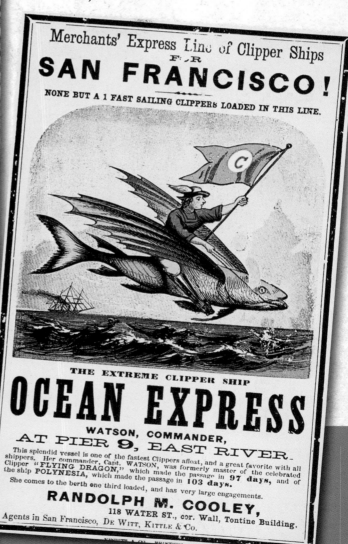

PERSPECTIVES

Look closely at this photograph from 1916. What materials did miners use to build retaining walls and sluice boxes? How did using these materials change the landscape you can see in the background? Is modern mining similar?

▶ Before railroads cut across the continent, people from the east wanting to get to the California goldfields had to sail around South America. Even without storm and rough seas, the journey would take about 60 days.

TYPES OF EVIDENCE

"A wise man... proportions his belief to the evidence."

David Hume, Scottish historian, 1748

Source material is the name we give to any collection of items that have been left behind from the past. Source materials can be things that are written, such as reports or letters; visual images such as maps, paintings, or photographs; or materials you hear such as music or recorded interviews. They are often kept in museums, online libraries, government **archives**, or private collections. Archives and museums are careful to protect documents from sunlight and heat or cold to make sure sources remain in good condition. Private collections sometimes contain **artifacts** or documents, handing them down for generations.

It is important to preserve source materials because they allow us to study and understand our past. Each bit of evidence adds another piece to the puzzle of what happened. Without source materials, we would never learn from past mistakes or successes. **Conservators** play a vital role in helping to restore them and keep them in good condition.

The two major gold rushes in North America were the California Gold Rush and the Klondike Gold Rush. But there were many smaller gold rushes, too. All of these events produced source materials. A lot of them are personal items. Miners sent letters, wrote diaries, took pictures, drew sketches, and kept artifacts. These things had meaning for them, so they were kept in families. Some artifacts are still being found at old mining sites. Recent construction in San Francisco has led to new artifacts being dug up. Chamber pots and toothbrushes made of bone and boar bristles found there give insight into life then.

▲ To raise money to buy mining equipment and **stake** claims, companies sold shares. At the time, ordinary people thought this was a way to share in the wealth of a gold mine. Most shares turned out to be worthless.

THE YUKON GOLDFIELDS
LIMITED.
INCORPORATED UNDER THE COMPANIES ACTS 1862 TO 1898.

CAPITAL £100,000.

DIVIDED INTO 100,000 SHARES OF £1 EACH.

FULLY PAID.

This is to Certify that _Neill Alexander Drummond Armstrong_ of _68 Grosvenor Road, Westminster_ is the Registered Proprietor of _Thirty-five_ Shares of One Pound each numbered as in the margin hereof in **THE YUKON GOLDFIELDS, LIMITED**, subject to the Memorandum and Articles of Association of the said Company and that up to this date there has been paid in respect of each of such Shares the sum of _Five Shillings_ Given under the Common Seal of the said Company this 15th day of January 1900

H. W. Forster

M. T. Armstrong

DIRECTORS.

...s will be Registered without the production of this Certificate.

N.B

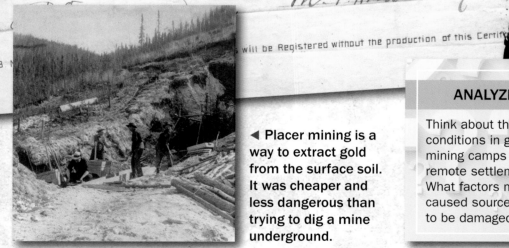

◀ Placer mining is a way to extract gold from the surface soil. It was cheaper and less dangerous than trying to dig a mine underground.

ANALYZE THIS

Think about the living conditions in gold mining camps and remote settlements. What factors might have caused source material to be damaged or lost?

HISTORICAL SOURCES

PRIMARY SOURCES

Source materials are sorted into how and when they were created. **Primary sources** are firsthand accounts or direct evidence of an event. They are usually created at the time of, or shortly after, an event happens. For individuals, primary sources can be material they created such as diaries, journals, or blogs, or that others created about them at the time, including photographs or reports made by family, friends, or co-workers.

There is a great deal of written primary source material for the gold rushes of North America. Thousands of people traveled to the site of a gold rush. They needed tickets for trains or boats to get them there. They wrote letters to their families to let them know where they were and that they were okay. Once they were in the area, they had to stake a claim. This involved registration forms or deeds if they bought land. Many men also kept diaries or journals of their adventure.

Some types of written sources are:
- Ticket stubs: the torn part of a ticket often shows the date, destination, and cost of ticket
- Diaries and journals: stories written down about daily life

- Newspapers: articles and photos reporting on daily events in a certain area
- Financial reports: documents for businesses showing gains and losses
- Advertisements: a flyer or space in a newspaper, magazine, or website to offer something for sale or rent
- Lyrics: the words of a song
- Letters: correspondence on paper between two people
- Social media: updates on social sites online

Diaries like the one written by John Sutter, pioneer of the California Gold Rush (see below), or by miner Bruce H. Wark, detail the difficulties men had in dealing with bad weather, broken sleighs, and crossing **waterways**. Wark wrote, "Tuesday, March 15, 1898. This is our busy day. Trouble without end. Water, water everywhere."

ANALYZE THIS

In the past, not everyone had the opportunity to go to school. Many people couldn't read or write. What primary sources might these people have created?

"'Intelligence,' he added, 'which if properly profited by would put both of us in possession of unheard-of-wealth—millions and millions of dollars, in fact.' ...when I heard this that I thought something had touched Marshall's brain, when suddenly all my misgivings were put at an end to by his flinging on the table a handful of scales of pure virgin gold."

John Sutter's diary, 1854

THE WESTERN UNION TELEGRAPH COMPANY.

INCORPORATED

21,000 OFFICES IN AMERICA.   CABLE SERVICE TO ALL THE WORLD.

Form No. 1.

This Company TRANSMITS and DELIVERS messages only on conditions limiting its liability, which have been assented to by the sender of the following message.
Errors can be guarded against only by repeating a message back to the sending station for comparison, and the Company will not hold itself liable for errors or delays
in transmission or delivery of Unrepeated Messages, beyond the amount of tolls paid thereon, nor in any case where the claim is not presented in writing within sixty days
after the message is filed with the Company for transmission.
This is an UNREPEATED MESSAGE, and is delivered by request of the sender, under the conditions named above.

THOS. T. ECKERT, President and General Manager.

NUMBER	SENT BY	REC'D BY	CHECK
5	H	Rm	50 Paid

RECEIVED at 9.15 Am   July 17, 1897

Dated Seattle Washington.

To Richard Pearce

News of wonderful richness of Klondyke northwest territory gold fields million dollars brought in last steamer excitement here similar California forty nine. Believe it ... me thirty days trip from ...

(7).

most interesting. You can from that form some idea of what our river travelling was like and can understand how I whose experience on rivers before was limited to the trip from Oxford to Henley have been through, in the months journey from Bennett to Dawson City an experience only equalled by those here with us and noted Explorers in unknown countries. I am splendidly well, have grown awfully fat, and when looked in a large mirror and saw a short filthy Specimen dressed in a worn out mackinaw coat, overalls and moccasins, with a full reddish beard, what little skin showing being almost as black as your hat I did not recognize your loving ... However four dollars expended at the Dawson City barber shop procured me bath, shave etc. and I was prepared to present with Bond our letters and take in the Situation. We first wished to get away from our camp at Louse town with the utmost speed as it was almost unbearable.

Diggings
Diggings Klondike
Cabin of Bond & Pearce

▲ Telegraphs were messages sent over a wire. This one shows the hope and excitement of striking it rich in the Klondike goldfield in the Yukon, Canada.

▶ Letters like this one to N. H. Pearce are often found in private collections. These source documents are saved because they have sentimental value to the family and contain a wealth of information about life during a gold rush.

SOURCES OF VISUAL EVIDENCE

Visual primary sources are the images created during or near the time of an event. Paintings are a way of seeing situations from the artists' points of view. The colors and lines can create a mood or feeling. They can make a statement about how an individual or society felt about an event, person, or place. Photographs capture a moment in time. They are a good way of comparing changes between the past and present.

Visual primary sources can include:

- Paintings: images made on canvas with paint
- Maps: diagrams of a region or area
- Posters: printed images with or without words
- Movies/Videos: moving images recorded by a camera
- Billboards: a large outdoor board showing advertisements
- Flyers/Brochures: small pamphlets with information about services or products

Photographs from the gold rushes show us the difficult conditions the miners faced. We can see the very rough and basic housing and equipment they struggled with in order to strike it rich. Pictures of miners with weather-beaten faces and chapped skin give us a clear idea of how hard life was for them. Maps

EVIDENCE RECORD CARD

Bodie State Historic Park
LEVEL Primary source
MATERIAL Color photograph
LOCATION Bodie Hills, Mono County, California
DATE 2016
SOURCE Shutterstock Images

▼ Gold mines have a lifespan. Once the gold runs out, or deposits are so small they are not worth mining, people leave. Towns that were thriving become **ghost towns**, like this one in Bodie State Historic Park, California.

from that time show how much of North America was still **uncharted** and how the gold rushes encouraged western settlement, taking much of the land from Indigenous peoples.

AUDITORY EVIDENCE

Interviews are a good **auditory** source of information. People who have lived through an event can talk about what it was like for them or give details that might not be found in reports. Music and songs give a glimpse into the **culture** of the time. Song lyrics reveal what was important to people. Recordings of the oral history and traditions of Indigenous peoples helps us understand the changes that came to their communities with the arrival of the miners and mining companies.

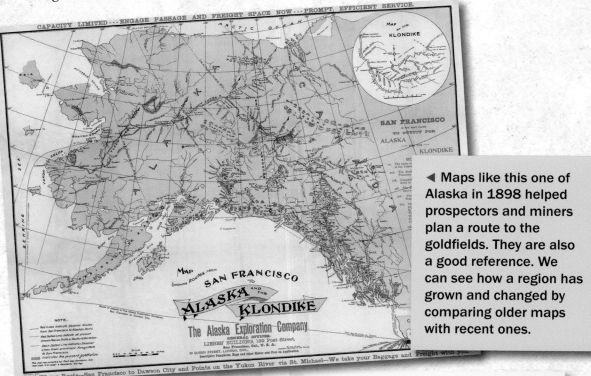

◀ Maps like this one of Alaska in 1898 helped prospectors and miners plan a route to the goldfields. They are also a good reference. We can see how a region has grown and changed by comparing older maps with recent ones.

ARTIFACTS AS PRIMARY EVIDENCE

Artifacts are also a source of information from the past. Items can detail how people lived, the effects of a natural disaster, or what technology was available then. Because there were many gold rushes across the continent, there are many artifacts to study. Handmade tools and machines give us an idea of the hard work involved. Gold pans, gold scales, and certificates remind us of the chance at a fortune that drove gold rushes. Miners' clothing indicate weather conditions.

SECONDARY SOURCES OF EVIDENCE

Secondary sources are evidence that is one step away from the actual event or person. They are often created by studying, discussing, or evaluating information found in primary sources. **Tertiary** sources are a further step away. They are not usually used for historical research, but rather as a way to find primary or secondary sources. They include directories and catalogs.

Novels that are set in the past are secondary sources. Through them we can learn details about that time. The story is often based on facts discovered in primary sources, especially diaries. Some secondary sources give a summary of an event, such as entries in a textbook or encyclopedia. Magazine articles are also mostly secondary sources. They rely on interviews or other documents. Movies about a certain historical person or event are a form of visual secondary source.

There have been many fiction and nonfiction books written on the gold rushes. Jack London wrote *The Call of the Wild* and *White Fang* after spending time in the Klondike chasing gold. His stories are based on what he saw and experienced there. *Klondike: The Last Great Gold Rush* by Pierre Berton is a nonfiction book that shares stories of interesting characters and wild adventures in the north. *The Life and Adventures of Joaquin Murieta* was a novel by Cherokee writer John Ridge published in 1854. It follows the adventures of a Mexican who travels to California during the gold rush. It is believed to be the first novel written by an Indigenous American.

One of the most famous poems about the gold rush in the Yukon is

▼ Jack London joined the gold rush to the Klondike in 1897. He had no success as a prospector or miner and returned to California where he used the Yukon as the setting for several articles and books.

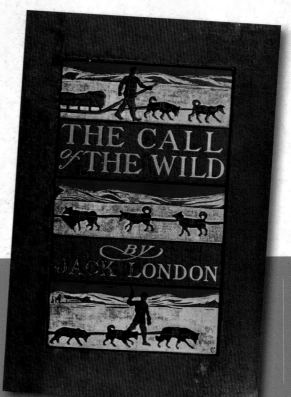

"There are strange things done in the midnight sun
    By the men who moil for gold;
The Arctic trails have their secret tales
    That would make your blood run cold;
The Northern Lights have seen queer sights,
    But the queerest they ever did see
Was that night on the marge of Lake Lebarge
    I cremated Sam McGee."

Robert W. Service

The *Cremation* of *Sam McGee* by Robert Service. It tells the story of a prospector who freezes to death and is cremated. It is based on a report of a man found dead in a cabin aboard a steamer ship in the Yukon.

The danger and excitement of striking it rich during the gold rushes were perfect for TV and movies. *City of Gold* (1957) and *The Far Country* are only two of many films made on the subject. Movies and TV shows can help viewers feel like they have traveled back in time to the gold rush days.

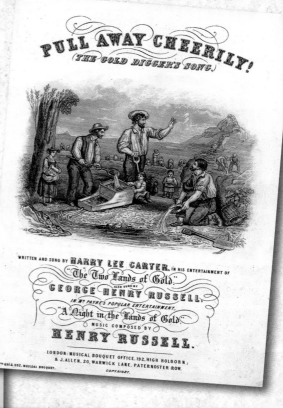

► The lyrics of the gold mining song "Pull Away, Cheerily," published in 1853, mentions the role of women. In the song, Sally helps by collecting gold **ore** in her apron while a small child plays nearby.

► This 1954 movie's fictional story of life during the Yukon gold rush focuses on lawlessness. It is loosely based on the tale of real-life con artist Soapy Smith who was based in Dyea and Skagway, Alaska. Smith and his gang duped miners out of their hard-earned cash.

PERSPECTIVES

Look closely at the book cover, movie poster, and songsheet cover. What impression do you get of the life of a gold miner from these images? Do they all give the same impression? How can looking at many different sources help us understand an event in the past?

INTERPRETATION

"Truth is universal. Perception of truth is not."

Anonymous

Source materials are created at different times, in different places, by different people. Just because they give information on a topic doesn't mean we should accept every detail as it is presented. That is because sources almost always have a **bias**. Bias is the personal opinion, viewpoint, or **prejudice** that all of us have. Everything we see, read, and create is affected by it. Bias is not necessarily bad, but we need to be aware of it when reading, viewing, or listening to source materials.

When reading source materials, historians also try to be aware of their own biases. They try to look at all evidence **critically** to give a balanced report. They consider the creators' points of view. They also try to compare each piece with other sources and reach a consensus of opinion.

During the California Gold Rush of 1848, the Chinese workers who were brought over from Asia to work were seen as a threat. They were paid lower wages—a practice that pitted other miners against them. When gold and jobs were scarce, they accused them of stealing their wealth. Images and diaries might show this bias by **portraying** the Chinese as sneaky or untrustworthy.

There was also bias against Indigenous peoples. They were considered by many at that time to be primitive and warlike. Paintings and sketches often portray them as threatening. Historic posters advertised the sale of "Indian Land." There was a common viewpoint among miners of that time that Indigenous land was free for the taking and **land treaties** could easily be ignored.

PERSPECTIVES

Look closely at this painting. Artists paint images from their **perspective**. Look at the setting, expression, and colors used. Using those details, what do you think the artist thought of the life of a gold miner?

▶ Henry Walton painted this picture called, "A Miner in His Cabin" in 1853. The man in the picture is identified as William D. Peck, a **Forty-niner** who went to California to make his fortune.

EVIDENCE RECORD CARD

California Gold Miner
LEVEL Primary source
MATERIAL Watercolor
LOCATION California goldfields
DATE 1853
SOURCE The Granger Collection

ANALYZING CONTEXT

As well as watching for bias in source materials, researchers need to be aware of **context**. Context is the setting in which an event occurs. Knowing what was going on in the area or the world at the time helps us to understand how people saw things. We can see how and why they acted or reacted to an event.

So what was the context of the time of the gold rushes? In California in 1848, the United States and Mexico were at war over the region. When a treaty was finally signed on February 2, 1848, gold had already been found, but this wasn't well known. If the value of the territory had been known, a treaty might not have been reached so quickly. In China, war and **famine** meant many men traveled to California to make money. They left their families behind and hoped to return wealthy. They had a positive outlook.

Before the Klondike Gold Rush started in 1896, the fur trade dominated the west and north of Canada. Fur traders and companies had routes, forts, and stores. The gold rush opened up new territory to outside prospectors and settlers, many of them from California. The Fraser River Gold Rush in British Columbia (1857-1865) led to other small

PERSPECTIVES

Look closely at the details in this painting of Chinese miners. How would you describe the miners based on these details? Do you think there is any bias in this image? Why or why not?

▼ Chinese immigrants who were no longer working for mining companies would often band together to buy or lease their own claims. They would work by hand to collect the gold left behind by bigger mining operations.

GROWING WITH THE LAST GREAT FRONTIER

THE WHITE PASS CHRONICLE

NEWS FROM THE KLONDIKE.

GOLD! GOLD! GOLD! GOLD!

Special Tug Chartered To Get The News.

WHITE HORSE TODAY

BUILDING BOOMING

White Horse, Apr. 1, 1901 — The spring boom has struck White Horse in earnest. The sound of hammers can be heard in all directions and vacant lots in the business portion of the town are becoming as scarce as mushrooms on an iceberg.

Many substantial frame buildings are going up, also many canvas ones which in time will give place to more permanent structures.

About 400 men are at present working in the town with the prospect of many more being employed, and in the evening the streets put one in mind of the great thoroughfares of the large cities throughout the states.

SKAGWAY AND UP RIVER POINTS

Alex Schwartz and Party Leave Bennett By Boat But Travel On Ice

Seattle, July 17, 1897. ON BOARD THE STEAMSHIP PORTLAND, 3:00 A.M. — At 3 o'clock this morning the steamship Portland, from St. Michaels for Seattle, passed up the Sound with more than a ton of solid gold on board and 68 passengers. In the captain's cabin are three chests and a large safe filled with the precious nuggets. The metal is worth nearly $700,000 and most of it was taken from the Klondike district in less than three months last winter. In size the nuggets range from the size of a pea to a guinea hen egg. Of the 68 miners on board hardly a man has less than $7,000, and one or two have more than $100,000 in yellow nuggets.

QUEEN VICTORIA

Clarence Berry is regarded as the luckiest man in the Klondike. Ten months ago he was a poor miner and to-day he is in Seattle with $130,000 in gold nuggets. One nugget ... ounce and is worth $231. "I've ...

The Land Of Gold

Showing the Yukon Country, With Klondike and Bonanza Creeks, Where

▶ Headlines like this one in *The White Pass Chronicle* fired up the imaginations of people desperate to become rich.

▼ Most of the people involved in the gold rushes were men. Women often worked as cooks, entertainers, and launderers.

gold rushes. These created conflicts with Indigenous peoples over land. Britain created the colony of British Columbia (1858-1866) to maintain control. British Columbia became a province of Canada in 1871.

Context of an event can help us understand how or why source materials were created. The large number of Chinese miners fleeing poverty in China and taking jobs in the mines led to political cartoons showing Chinese workers as a threat. Indigenous peoples fighting for their land and their rights were shown in paintings and sketches as the enemy. Photographs in newspapers of goldfields sometimes showed harsh conditions for workers.

"The little Kanaka woman lives here. I went to see her. She is quite pretty, with large lustrous eyes, and two great braids of hair which made me think of black satin cables, they were so heavy and massive. She has good teeth, a sweet smile, and a skin not much darker than that of a French brunette. I never saw any creature so proud as she...was of her baby."

Louise Clapp letter from California mines, 1851–1852.

GOLD RUSHES

"Genius is the gold in the mine; talent is the miner who works and brings it out."

Irish author, Marguerite Gardiner,
Countess of Blessington, 1855

A gold rush can happen anywhere a new **deposit** of gold is found and a wave of people come to make their fortune. Mining wasn't always thought to be the best way to make money. It was dangerous, hard work. Farming was more of a sure thing. But gold mining had something other ordinary jobs did not—the chance to become rich quickly and move up in society. Many were willing to take the chance on mining in order to change their **status**. The fact was that only a few made their fortune. Many left with nothing. The people supplying miners or offering transportation to the goldfields often made the most money.

The first significant gold rush in North America was in North Carolina in 1799. Twelve-year-old Conrad Reed was fishing in a creek on his family's farm when he found a huge gold rock. It turned out to be a 17-pound (7.7-kg) gold nugget. Word spread and locals started looking on the ground and in creeks for their own treasure. But everything changed when Matthias Barringer found that gold is often in the veins of white **quartz**. The focus moved from placer mining (panning) to lode, or underground, mining. Mining companies bought up land and brought in mining experts from around the world. At one mine in Charlotte, North Carolina, the diverse workforce spoke 13 different languages. The experts shared new technology, settled with their families, and forever changed the cultural makeup of the area.

Look closely at this miners' poster. How many of the images do you think are accurate and how many just look like ideas people had of what life was like in the early goldfields? Would this poster have tempted you to join a gold rush? Why, or why not?

SPAKE THESE WORDS, AND SAID: I am ...andered from "Away Down East," and came to ...ange land and "See the Elephant." And behold ... bear witness that, from the key of his trunk to ...tail, his whole body has passed before me; and I ...until his huge feet stood still before a clapboard ...ith his trunk extended, he pointed to a candlecard ... shingle, as though he would say **"READ!"**

...RS' TEN COMMANDMENTS.

I.

...alt have no other claim than one.

II.

...alt not make unto thyself any false claim, nor any ... mean man by jumping one. Whatever thou findest, ...k, or I will visit the miners around to invite them ... and when they decide against thee, thou shalt take ... pan, the shovel, and thy blankets, with all that ...nd go prospecting to seek good diggings; but thou ...one. Then, when thou hast returned, in sorrow ...ind that thine old claim is worked out, and yet no ...ee to hide in the ground or in an old boot beneath ... in buckskin or bottle underneath thy cabin; but ... that was in thy purse away, worn out thy boots and ...s, so that there is nothing good about them but the ...d thy patience is likened unto thy garments; and at ...alt hire thy body out to make thy board and save

III.

...shalt not go prospecting before thy claim gives out. ...alt thou take thy money, nor thy gold dust, nor thy ... to the gaming table in vain; for monte, twenty-one, ...aro, lansquenet and poker will prove to thee that the ...puttest down the less thou shalt take up; and when ...est of thy wife and children, thou shalt not hold ...iftless, but—insane.

IV.

...shalt not remember what they friends do at home on ...th day, lest the remembrance may not compare favor- ...what thou doest here. Six days thou mayest dig or ...hat thy body can stand under, but the other day is ... yet thou washest all thy dirty shirts, darnest all thy ..., tap thy boots, mend thy clothing, chop thy whole ...re-wood, make up and bake thy bread and boil thy ... beans that thou wait not when thou returnest from thy ... weary. For in six days' labor only thou canst not ...ough to wear out thy body in two years; but if thou ... hard on Sunday also, thou canst do it in six months; ... and thy son and thy daughter, thy male and thy female ...y morals and thy conscience be none the less better for ...eproach thou shouldst thou ever return to thy mother's ...and thou strive to justify thyself because the trader and

the blacksmith, the carpenter and the merchant, the tailors, Jews and Buccaneers defy God and civilization by keeping not the Sabbath day, nor wish for a day of rest, such as memory of youth and home made hallowed.

V.

Thou shalt not think more of all thy gold, nor how thou canst make it fastest, than how thou wilt enjoy it after thou hast ridden rough-shod over thy good old parents' precepts and ex- amples, that thou mayest have nothing to reproach and sting thee when thou art left alone in the land where thy father's blessing and thy mothers's love hath sent thee.

VI.

Thou shalt not kill thy body by working in the rain, even though thou shalt make enough to buy physic and attendance with. Neither shalt thou kill thy neighbor's body in a duel, for by keeping cool thou canst save his life and thy conscience. Neither shalt thou destroy thyself by getting "*tight*," nor "*slewed*," nor "*high*," nor "*corned*," nor "*half-seas over*," nor "*three sheets in the wind*," by drinking smoothly down nor "*brandy slings*," "*gin cock-tails*," "*whisky punches*," "*rum toddies*" nor "*egg nogs*." Neither shalt thou suck "*mint juleps*" nor "*sherry cobblers*" through a straw, nor gurgle from a bottle the raw material, nor take it neat from a decanter, for while thou art swallowing down thy purse and thy coat from off thy back, thou art burning the coat from off thy stomach; and if thou couldst see the houses and lands, and gold dust, and home comforts already lying there—a huge pile—thou shouldst feel a choking in thy throat; and when to that thou add'st thy crooked walking and hiccupping ; of lodging in the gutter, and broiling in the sun, of prospect holes half full of water, and of shafts and ditches from which thou hast emerged like a drown- ing rat, thou wilt feel disgusted with thyself, and inquire, "*Is thy servant a dog that he doeth these things?*" Verily, I will say, farewell old bottle! I will kiss thy gurgling lips no more; and thou, slings, cock-tails, punches, smashes, cobblers, nogs, toddies, sangarees and juleps, forever, farewell. Thy remem- brance shames me; henceforth I will cut thy acquaintance; and headaches, tremblings, heart-burnings, blue-devils, and all the unholy catalogue of evils which follow in thy train. My wife's smiles and my children's merry-hearted laugh shall charm and reward me for having the manly firmness and courage to say: "*No! I wish thee an eternal farewell!!*"

VII.

Thou shalt not grow discouraged, nor think of going home before thou hast made thy "*pile*," because thou hast not "*struck a lead*" nor found a rich "*crevice*" nor sunk a hole upon a "*pocket*," lest in going home thou leave four dollars a day and go to work ashamed at fifty cents a day, and serve thee right; for thou knowest by staying here thou mightest strike a lead and fifty dollars a day, and keep thy manly self-respect, and then go home with enough to make thyself and family happy.

VIII.

Thou shalt not steal a pick, or a pan, or a shovel ... fellow miner, nor take away his tools without his ... borrow those he cannot spare; nor return them be... trouble him to fetch them back again; nor talk with ... his water rent is running on; nor remove his stake ... thy claim; nor undermine his claim in following a lea... out gold from his riffle-box; nor wash the tailings ... mouth of his sluices. Neither shalt thou pick out ... from the company's pan to put in thy mouth or in ... nor cheat thy partner of his share; nor steal from ... mate his gold dust to add to thine, for he will be ... cover what thou hast done, and will straightway call his fellow miners together, and if the law hinder them not they will hang thee, or give thee fifty lashes, or shave thy head and brand thee like a horse thief with "R" upon thy cheek, to be known and of all men Californians in particular.

IX.

Thou shalt not tell any false tales about "*good diggings in the mountains*" to thy neighbor, that thou mayest benefit a friend who hath mules, and provisions, and tools, and blankets he cannot sell; lest in deceiving thy neighbor when he returns through the snow, with naught but his riffle, he present thee with the contents thereof, and like a dog thou shalt fall down and die.

X.

Thou shalt not commit unsuitable matrimony, nor covet "*single blessedness*," nor forget absent maidens, nor neglect thy first love; but thou shalt consider how faithfully and patiently she waiteth thy return; yea, and covereth each epistle that thou sendeth with kisses of kindly welcome until she hath return. Neither shalt thou covet thy neighbor's wife, nor trifle with the affections of his daughter; yet, if thy heart be free, and thou love and covet each other, thou shalt "*pop the question*" like a man, lest another more manly than thou art should step in be- fore thee, and thou lovest her in vain, and, in the anguish of thy heart's disappointment, thou shalt quote the language of the great, and say, "*sick is life*;" and thy future lot be that of a poor, lonely, despised and comfortless bachelor.

A new commandment give I unto you. If thou hast a wife and little ones, that thou lovest dearer than thy life, that thou keep them continually before you to cheer and urge thee onward until thou canst say, "*I have enough; God bless them; I will return.*" Then as thou journiest towards thy much loved home, with open arms, shall they come forth to welcome thee, and falling on thy neck, weep tears of unutterable joy that thou art come; then in the fullness of thy heart's gratitude thou shalt kneel before thy Heavenly Father together, to thank Him for thy safe return. Amen. So mote it be.

SCENES WHEN CROSSING THE PLAINS IN 1849.

THE MINERS' PIONEER TEN COMMANDMENTS

▲ Life was very different in the goldfields from what people were used to at home. Posters such as this one would be hung on the wall to help newcomers adjust to their new life.

CALIFORNIA GOLD RUSH

The first major North American gold rush started in 1848. In January of that year James Marshall was building a lumber mill in Coloma, California. At that time California was governed by Mexico. He found shiny metal in the waterway and took it to the owner of the mill, John Sutter. They tested it and found out it was gold. Sutter wanted to keep the news quiet, but rumors started to spread. At about March—by which time California was under American control—the news of the discovery had spread across the country, and soon more than 80,000 people moved to the area to mine.

In May 1848 a **merchant** named Samuel Brannan realized that while he might not find treasure himself, he could still make money from mining. He loaded his store with equipment for miners and ran through the streets shouting, "Gold! Gold! Gold from the American River!" Newspaper articles reported that gold was so plentiful it could be scooped up by the handful from the ground.

The California Gold Rush started with prospectors coming from Oregon, Hawaii, and Latin America. Later, miners came from Europe, Australia, and China. About half came by sea; the rest came by land on the California Trail. This route followed rivers and streams and finally crossed the Sierra Nevada Mountains into northern California. Because California was not yet a state with its own laws—that happened in 1850—the gold was "free for the taking." There was no private property, no licensing fees, and no taxes. Many of the immigrants that had made the long and difficult journey saw gold mining as a way to easy money and a new life. The economy of the United States—and not Mexico—was boosted, and Brannan himself went on to become California's first millionaire.

"The gold is here, but if we can make more by digging potatoes, they are the surest business."

Colonel Isaac T. Avery, Burke County, to William B. Lenoir, February 22, 1829

AN ACCOUNT OF

CALIFORNIA,

AND THE

WONDERFUL GOLD REGIONS.

A New Arrival at the Gold Diggings.

WITH A DESCRIPTION OF

The Different Routes to California;

Information about the Country, and the Ancient and Modern Discoveries of Gold;

How to Test Precious Metals; Accounts of Gold Hunters;

TOGETHER WITH MUCH OTHER

Useful Reading for those going to California, or having Friends there.

ILLUSTRATED WITH MAPS AND ENGRAVINGS.

BOSTON:

PUBLISHED BY J. B. HALL, 66 CORNHILL.
For Sale at Skinner's Publication Rooms, 60½ Cornhill.

Price, 12½ cents.

ANALYZE THIS

At the time of the California Gold Rush in 1848, North America was very different in terms of communication, travel, and laws. If another major gold find happened today, how would the gold rush be different? Who would benefit the most?

▶ Some gold strikes were made by prospectors searching likely areas. The gold at Sutter's Mill that started the California Gold Rush was found by accident.

◀ Many people made money during the gold rushes from other businesses. Publishers sold gold-mining guidebooks to prospectors. They gave information on routes to the goldfields, how to mine, and what animals they might encounter.

"Inexhaustible Gold Mines in California: The intelligence from California, that gold can be picked up in lumps, weighing six or seven ounces, and scooped up in tin pans at the rate of a pound of the pure dust a scoop, whilst rich supplies of quicksilver, platina, etc, are so plentiful as to be entirely neglected for the more precious metal, has set the inhabitants of this great republic almost crazy."

California Herald newspaper, December 26, 1848

GOLD RUSH BOOMTOWN

The California Gold Rush left a lasting mark on the region. With the Forty-niners flowing in, entire Indigenous societies were pushed from their land. In documents and advertisements, the land was referred to as "empty." The villages, hunting grounds, ceremonial and burial grounds were trampled on, cleared off, and built over. Early settlers believed in Manifest Destiny: the idea that **expansion** and settlement in the North American West was the right of Americans with European ancestors. They didn't feel the need to ask permission or worry about what would happen to Indigenous peoples. Violence and disease

ANALYZE THIS

What source material might exist to give information about the Indigenous peoples affected by the gold rushes? Did Indigenous peoples pass down their histories and cultures mostly in written or story-telling form? How might this affect how their history is recorded, studied, and analyzed by others?

▼ For many prospectors eager to join the California Gold Rush, the fastest way there was by sea. In 1849 alone, about 25,000 prospectors arrived by ship.

killed off a third of the region's 150,000 or more American Indians.

The crush of people needing food, shelter, and supplies caused cities like Sacramento and San Francisco to grow. Ships from around the world brought supplies to San Francisco. Most passengers and many of the crews left the ships to seek their fortune in the goldfields. The harbor was full of abandoned ships. Eventually people began to take the ships apart and use the lumber to build new stores, hotels, and jails. The landscape also changed. Rivers were dammed and **diverted**. High-pressure water hoses were used to wash away cliffs. New roads cut through ancient forests and new towns sprung up in remote areas.

In 1850 California became the 31st state in the Union. The new government passed a Foreign Miner's Tax. People coming from other states or countries had to pay $20 each, every month, in order to mine. That would be about $500 a month in today's money. That law was struck down and a new law came in its place. Now only Chinese miners had to pay. This was because of the prejudice against them. Although they were charged $2 a month (about $50 today), that was a lot for poorly paid people.

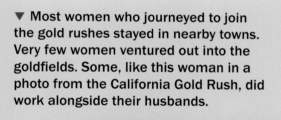

▼ Most women who journeyed to join the gold rushes stayed in nearby towns. Very few women ventured out into the goldfields. Some, like this woman in a photo from the California Gold Rush, did work alongside their husbands.

EVIDENCE RECORD CARD

California gold rush

LEVEL Primary source
MATERIAL Black-and-white photograph
LOCATION California
DATE 1850s
SOURCE Topfoto Images

FRASER RIVER GOLD RUSH

Just as the California Gold Rush changed that state, the Fraser River, or Fraser Canyon Gold Rush changed British Columbia. It was not a large or long rush, but it had a lasting impact. In 1857 gold was found in a **tributary** of the Fraser River. When news reached San Francisco, miners from the California Gold Rush were excited. Many had failed to make their fortune in California. They saw the Fraser Canyon as a new hope for riches. Tens of thousands began flooding the city of Victoria, British Columbia. The governor of the **colony** of British Columbia tried to control the rush. He wanted to limit the number of weapons brought into the area. He made it law that everyone entering British Columbia had to come by way of Victoria. But many miners traveled overland across old trails. Prospectors spread out all over the river valleys searching for gold.

The sudden arrival of so many people into the Fraser River Canyon had a devastating effect on Indigenous people in the region. The miners not only claimed land wherever they wanted, but they also brought disease. There was also prejudice and racism that led to many conflicts.

▼ Gold is often found in remote areas. Narrow, winding mountain passes were dangerous. Criminals would wait to ambush miners or stagecoaches carrying gold.

"It has been rumoured that the Hudson's Bay Company are wishful to deter American Citizens from mining in this region; now if I may advance my humble opinion I think it is very unpolitic and grievously wrong, for every Englishman in California has the same privilege in mining as any American citizen."

Letter from B. H. Hunter, originally of Whitby, Yorkshire, England, to Right Honorable Henry Stanley, Colonial Office, London, England, May 5, 1858

An article in the *Chilliwack Progress* newspaper in 1904 revealed that after the gold rush, white miners who had become ranchers and farmers in California had abducted Indigenous Stó:lo boys. They took them back to California and forced them to work. Some returned as grown men but most were never seen again.

The problems created by the gold rush resulted in growth and changes. New roads and towns were built. New laws were created to try to build up the territory while avoiding conflicts and violence. The foundations that were laid during this time led to the colony becoming the sixth province of Canada, in 1871.

ANALYZE THIS

The gold rushes led to the creation of many new laws. What do you think these related to? Why were they essential? What can we learn by studying how and why laws were created? What bias should we look for?

▼ Prospectors could not carry all their food, clothing, and equipment themselves. They used pack animals, mainly horses, to help them get what they needed to the goldfields. They would have to leave their horses behind at the Chilkoot Pass because it was too steep for horses.

Mining Prospectors with pack horses Northern British Columbia.

T. N. Hibben & Co., Victoria, British Columbia Nº 51.

LAND GRABS, LAW, AND ORDER

There were many smaller gold rushes all around North America. Big or small, gold rushes forever changed the area where gold was found. The Dahlonega Gold Rush in Georgia saw thousands of prospectors coming to claim land and get rich. The men, women, and children of the Cherokee Nation living there were powerless to stop the invasion. In an Indigenous newspaper, the *Cherokee Phoenix*, one Cherokee said, "Our neighbors who regard no law and pay no respects to the laws of humanity are now reaping a plentiful harvest…We are an abused people." But miners kept coming and digging holes in the ground.

When gold ran out in one goldfield, miners went looking for another **pay streak** nearby. They brought new mining technology with them. They also brought their habits and traditions, good and bad. When gold was first discovered in Alder **Gulch**, Montana, in 1863, the prospectors tried to keep the discovery quiet. They had learned from other gold rushes to keep the news of the discovery —and so the gold—to themselves. But word got out, and over a few months tens of thousands moved in. Soon settlements lined the gulch. The area became known as "Fourteen Mile City."

▲ Underground mining was risky. This cross-section shows the structures built to support the ceilings and walls as a mine expanded. Many miners lost their lives due to cave-ins, wooden beams collapsing, or poisonous gases.

"We went up Boot Hill, and ate in a tavern. I guess I expected to find an old bar with gold scales, and miners paying for drinks in dust. Instead, we found a 'quick and dirty' with Coca Cola signs and no atmosphere."

Charles Bovey on his arrival in 1944 at Virginia City, which had developed from a gold-mining settlement 80 years ealier

ANALYZE THIS

Towns like Virginia City were created and grew rapidly. What problems can arise when a settlement grows quickly? What problems can there be for towns depending on one industry?

The tents and cabins eventually combined into two larger cities only 1 mile (1.6 km) apart: Virginia City and Nevada City. Virginia City became the capital of the territory. City planners tried to have it grow along a grid. However, miners built cabins wherever they wanted. This boomtown had no sheriffs to keep crime under control. It became known for the robberies and murders along the trails. Crime was a problem in many remote areas where gold rushes occurred. A civilian group known as the Montana **Vigilantes** began patrolling and punishing gang members until 1864, when the first judge arrived.

▶ Deadwood, South Dakota, was established in 1876 during the Black Hills Gold Rush. Much of the mining in this area was underground mining for lode gold.

KLONDIKE GOLD RUSH

Indigenous people in the Klondike area of the Yukon, Canada, had known for a long time that there was gold. To them it was not as useful a metal as copper because it was so soft. But when George Carmack, Kate Carmack, Skookum Jim, and Dawson Charlie saw the gold glitter in Rabbit Creek on August 16, 1896, they knew they were about to strike it rich. The next day they staked their claims.

They made the long journey to Forty Mile to register the claim. The first name on the form reads, "Tagish, Jim (Indian), September 24, 1896." Word spread all up and down the Yukon River. Miners who were mining in the surrounding area came rushing in to stake any claim they could along the river, its tributaries, and any other small creeks. Rabbit Creek was soon renamed **Bonanza** Creek.

The news of the find didn't reach the outside world until the following summer. In July when **river steamers** could finally sail the thawed rivers, the miners took their gold down the west coast to sell it. By the time the steamer *Excelsior* docked in San Francisco, it had about $500,000 worth of gold on board.

PERSPECTIVES

Candid photographs are those taken without people posing. They capture a moment in time as it happened, such as this black-and-white photo from Dawson City in about 1897. Are photographs like this primary or secondary sources? What information can we learn by looking at historic images?

▼ The construction business in cities like Dawson City during the Klondike Gold Rush was booming. Men made a lot of money cutting lumber and building cabins and stores for the miners.

When the *Portland* arrived in Seattle three days later, reporters were ready. Newspaper headlines announced "half a ton of gold" on board.

Now the gold rush was on. Tens of thousands of people headed north. They didn't understand the difficulties or dangers of traveling or working in the Yukon. There was very little written about what it was like. It wouldn't have mattered—the excitement was running so high, most would have ignored the warnings anyway. The United States had just suffered a series of bank failures and people were desperate for money. More than 100,000 men tried to make the journey. Only 30,000 to 40,000 made it.

▼ This Canadian prospector's license was issued to F. Crouch of Staplecross, England, on March 2, 1898, during the Klondike Gold Rush. The license cost $10 and allowed Crouch to mine for a year as well as to shoot and fish.

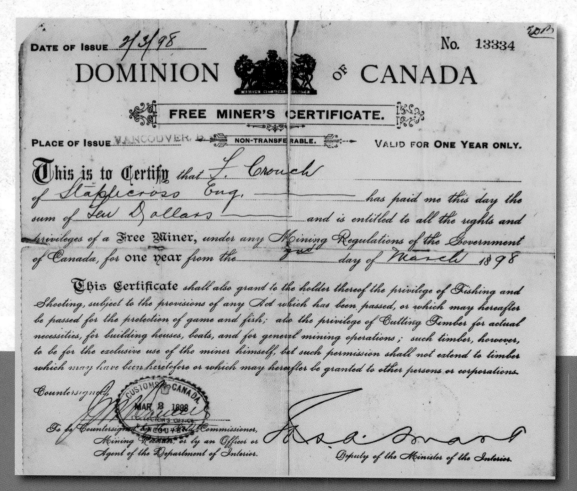

KLONDIKE JOURNEY

In October 1897 a book called *Klondike: A Manual for Goldseekers* was published. In it, new miners were advised to "imitate the Indians in dress and habit. It is useless to wear leather or gum boots. Good **moccasins** are absolutely necessary." It told them what to expect from the climate and the landscape. An all-water journey from the Pacific upriver to Dawson was called the "rich-man's route" because it was so expensive. Most men traveled part of the way by ship and then they had to go on foot the rest of the way over high mountain passes. Miners who landed in Dyea, Alaska, had to use the Chilkoot Trail to get to Bennett, British Columbia. The steepest part was called "The Golden Stairs." At the bottom

▶ **Prospectors and miners on the dangerous trek up the 1,500 steps of the Golden Stairs at Chilkoot Pass. They had to carry all their supplies and equipment. It was too rough for horses.**

ANALYZE THIS

Source material has been created as long as humans have written, painted, or **sculpted**. What primary sources might the prospectors have used to learn about this foreign place, mining, or how to succeed?

"Our great drawback is the lack of ready cash. Instead of arriving here with three or four thousand dollars as we expected to do—we were almost out of cash when we got here. Then we had to buy a cabin, get more grub, lay in firewood etc. etc. at exorbitant prices....I do hope we will be successful, as one surely deserves a great deal of recompense for what we have gone through."

Letter from Stanley H. Pearce in the Klondike to his mother in Colorado, December 16, 1897

was a weighing station known as "The Scales." Some men saw how steep and dangerous the snow-covered Golden Staircase was and gave up. They left all their equipment at The Scales. Because of the cold temperatures, many artifacts were preserved right where they were dropped. We can study them today.

By law each man had to bring with him enough food to last a year. That would weigh about 1,000 pounds (454 kg). Their mining equipment could weigh another 1,000 pounds. Many brought pack animals or sleds to help carry everything. Others hired Indigenous men to help

▼ Most prospectors walked for days along trails and through the mountains to get to the Klondike. Men with more money could hire ice motors to traveled in.

them carry their goods. Owners of sleds and pack animals as well as Indigenous packers would often demand even higher prices here. Once over the mountains, the miners would have to sail more than 600 miles (966 km) downriver to Dawson.

Before the gold rush in 1896, Dawson City didn't even exist. In 1897 there were about 5,000 people living there. The next year there were some 30,000. People came from all over the world. Claims were first staked at the site. Then miners had three days to register the claim in Dawson. If a miner left a claim for more than three days without a good reason, another person could legally claim it. Of the many thousands of people who raced to the Klondike, only a few hundred became rich.

on the Klondyke River

Ice Motor on Way to Dawson, Yukon, or British Territory.

NOT ALL WAS GOLDEN

"During the Gold Rush, most would-be miners lost money, but people who sold them picks, shovels, tents and blue-jeans made a nice profit."

Peter Lynch, American investor, 2000

The life of gold miners during a gold rush was very different from what they were used to and from what they expected when they set out to find riches. Coins and bills were rare in the Klondike. Photographs show miners paying for bread with gold dust. It was worth about $16 dollars an ounce (28 g). Today it is worth about $1,280 per ounce. Most couldn't find a cabin to live in. Rent was extremely high and the price of lumber to build one cost twenty times what it did farther south. The food was terrible— mostly beans and rancid bacon and beef jerky—and expensive. Gambling was common and an easy way to lose money. Many men weren't finding enough gold to live on. Newspaper ads show that some were willing to trade part-ownership of their claims for food and supplies.

Many of the people who made good money during the gold rushes didn't mine at all. They were the people providing services to the miners. Anyone who owned a boat used it to transport miners and their equipment to the goldfields. Others rented pack animals. Some built **tramways** at the Golden Stairs to lift tons of gear up over the heads of weary men struggling up the trail.

In town there were many businesses making money off the prospectors and miners. Hotels, restaurants, and dance halls kept prospectors and miners housed and fed. Saloons were open around the clock. Although women were rare, some came to work as cooks, teachers, nurses, or even dancers. In her diary, L. B. May wrote on March 31, 1897, that they even had a woman doctor in town.

▶ This political cartoon was published in *Puck* magazine in September 1897. It showed a miner surrounded by others trying to make a profit off of him. Some of the vultures are labeled gin mill keeper, gambling den, dive keeper, and dance housekeeper.

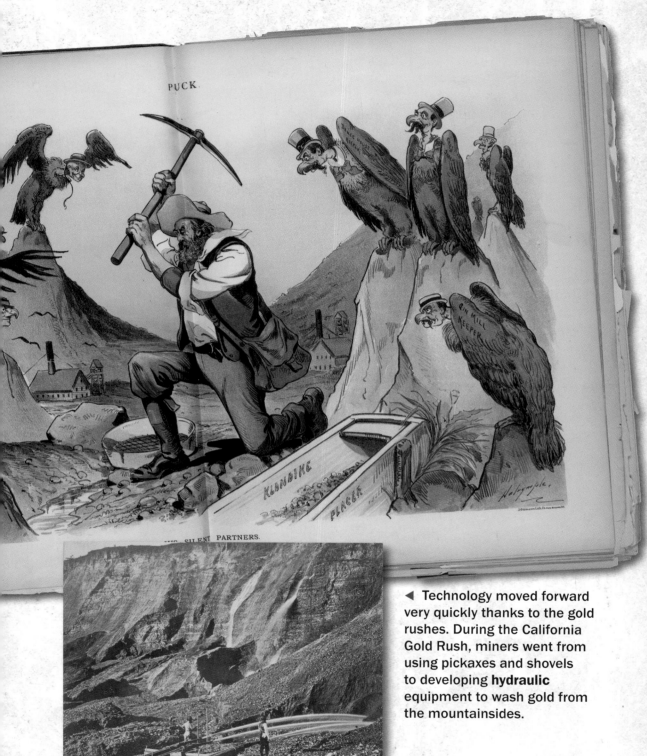

◀ Technology moved forward very quickly thanks to the gold rushes. During the California Gold Rush, miners went from using pickaxes and shovels to developing **hydraulic** equipment to wash gold from the mountainsides.

LAW AND ORDER

The possibility of great and instant wealth often brought out the worst in people. Claim jumping was a problem in the goldfields. This involved someone other than the first person to stake the claim grabbing it for themselves. Sometimes the jumper would simply pull out the first miner's stakes, put in their own, and beat them to the **land recorder's office** to register. Occasionally, a claim jumper would simply mine land without staking a claim at all. The jumper would sneak onto the property and start digging or force off the claim owner.

With so much gold dust, gold bars, or gold nuggets being stored or carried, robbery was always a danger. The goldfields were mostly in remote, **isolated** areas with empty roads through forests or valleys and no

PERSPECTIVES

Look closely at this black-and-white photograph of **con man** Jefferson "Soapy" Smith. He is posing in a saloon in Skagway, Alaska. Look at the details of his clothing, hair, and pose. What impression do you think he is trying to make? Who is he trying to influence? Do people always portray themselves accurately in photos? Should you be careful when making judgments about people or events based on one photograph? Why or why not?

◀ Jefferson "Soapy" Smith was a con man in Skagway, Alaska. He swindled miners in saloons, in gambling dens, and by operating fake telegraph offices. He died in a shootout in Juneau, Alaska, in July 1898.

"Clothing of all descriptions strews the ground all over. Left by those that have camped here and gone to the mines. Shirts never worn but once or twice are thrown away rather than pay for washing. 50 cts is the charge for washing a piece or $6 per dozen and no less—so collars boosoms (sic) etc. are thrown away indiscriminately. I have seen pants whole and sound and but little soiled thrown away."

Letter from Hiram Dwight Pierce to his wife Sara Jane Pierce, San Francisco, California, October 18, 1849

protection. Greed and jealousy led to murders and theft.

In some areas vigilante groups formed to protect miners. The Montana Vigilantes who protected the miners of Alder Gulch moved with the miners when gold was found in Helena, Montana. There they were called the Helena Committee of Safety. They dealt with crimes of horse stealing, murder, and highway robbery.

In the Klondike in Canada, the North-West Mounted Police (NWMP) kept the peace. They escorted prospectors and miners through dangerous river rapids near Whitehorse. They also traveled with gold shipments from the goldfields to the banks in Dawson City. But the population had grown so large so quickly that the NWMP force was too small to support so many people. A special force was pulled from Canada's **militia** and called the Yukon Field Force. They helped guard prisoners, banks, and gold shipments. Colonel Sam Steele of the NWMP set the rule that miners had to bring a year's supply of goods to support themselves. Steele was known as tough but fair and understood he had to have a firm hand with unruly miners. He and his force ensured that there was law and order in the Klondike, which make it unusal among gold rushes .

▶ Wells Fargo Bank started by opening offices in towns and mining camps like those of the Klondike goldfields. Wells Fargo took over the western portion of the Pony Express mail delivery service. Both companies grew thanks to the needs of people in the mining industry.

◀ Pony Express Postmark, 1860

ANALYZE THIS

Were all miners well-off and well-educated? What different backgrounds might they have had? Do you think some were easily taken advantage of by con men and criminals? Why or why not?

HISTORY REPEATED

"The first treasure California began to surrender after the Gold Rush was the oldest: her land."

John Jakes, American writer, 2012

The gold rushes left lasting changes in North America. In the panic to claim land and find gold, prospectors and miners swarmed onto Indigenous lands. They crossed trails without respecting treaties already in place, and they claimed land that was already being used by others. Mining **disrupted** animal habitats and herd migrations by redirecting rivers and digging up the ground.

Gold rushes brought settlers who established homesteads in remote areas. People gathered in these new locations to found cities such as Skagway, Dawson City, and Whitehorse. Once these remote areas were opened up, other minerals and **natural resources** were found. This led to more mines, pits, and wells to collect these valuable **reserves**. Railroads, highways, and steamship services expanded. States provinces, and territories were created and joined to enlarge and strengthen the United States and Canada. The invention of new technologies was driven by the miners' desire to mine faster, deeper, and more efficiently.

The **inflow** of so many immigrants from other countries altered the ethnic makeup of North America. Asians, South Americans, Australians, Africans, and Europeans brought their languages and customs. Those who stayed on after the gold rushes added to the history of North America.

▶ The Barrick Goldstrike mine in Nevada is the largest gold mine in North America. There are both open-pit and underground mines there. It has more than 3,000 employees.

Mining has led to **permanent** changes to the remote areas where gold was found and a gold rush started. Melting Arctic ice means mineral-rich land is opening up in the far north of North America. What rules should be in place to protect the environment and culture of Indigenous people living in the area, based on what we have learned by looking back at previous gold rushes?

GOLD MINING TODAY

Gold mining has changed a lot since the days of the gold rushes. While there are still some individual miners on private property or small claims, most gold mining today in North America is done by large corporations. Millions of dollars are spent on complicated **sluices**, massive haul trucks, and powerful excavators. Demand for gold is higher than ever. It is used for many things including jewelry, currency, and electronics such as cell phones, televisions, and computers.

Most big mining companies operate mines all over the world. In some areas, laws that govern conditions for workers, and the environment, are weak. Some mining companies take advantage of the lack of protections. These companies have been accused of **human rights abuses**. They have dumped chemicals and garbage into the only drinking water of nearby villages. They do not create safe workplaces. Security guards have used violence against workers and those living near the mines. Just like the original goldfields during the gold rushes, these mines can be miserable and violent. There are labor strikes, robberies, and even murders as people struggle to make money and be treated fairly.

Towns that form near gold mines are often in remote areas and rely on only one industry—mining. The gold eventually runs out. Many towns are abandoned and become ghost towns. They sometimes leave behind a scarred landscape and polluted soil and water. In some places, laws force mine owners to return the land to its natural state when mines are closed. They have to make sure nearby water is not being polluted by **mine tailings**.

▲ The Mount Kare gold mine in Papua New Guinea has a rich gold deposit. While the mining project has brought roads and power lines into the area, workers are still digging in dangerous conditions using simple tools and no safety equipment.

"There's a number of other projects throughout the Yukon that are quite promising. So I think it's a favourable government situation here, and right now a favourable currency situation... it certainly bodes well for the Yukon."

Bill Sheriff, interview with James West, May 17, 2016

They have to put back the topsoil that they stripped off and replant trees and shrubs.

Gold mining is still affecting Indigenous peoples. Often, like the early gold rushes, their rights are ignored in the race to grab land and water. Governments use the military to protect mining companies. Mining companies also hire private security companies to threaten and sometimes harm people who oppose them. Canada is home to more than half of the world's mining companies. The United Nations has urged Canada to press these companies to respect human rights in the countries they operate in.

▼ Gold has even more uses today than in the past. Gold is a vital part of computers. Almost all electronics, from cell phones to tablets, contain gold.

PERSPECTIVES

Look at the image of miners in the Papua New Guinea gold mine. What conditions are these miners working in? What dangers can you see? Why do you think they are not using the modern technolgy or safety equipment that mines in North America have?

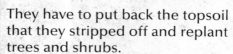

TIMELINE

1799 Gold discovered in North Carolina, creating the first U.S. gold rush

1800

1828 Dahlonega, Georgia, gold rush starts

January 1848 James Marshall finds gold at Sutter's Mill in California

March 1848 *The Californian* newspaper reports gold find

November 1848 First gold ship, carrying $500,000, leaves San Francisco for U.S. **Mint**

1849 Ninety thousand hopeful people, known as the "Forty-niners," arrive in California

June 1849 First gold miners who sailed around Cape Horn arrive in San Fransisco

April 1850 California begins to tax foreign miners

1850

September 1850 California becomes a U.S. state

May 1852 Second miners' tax passed, this time aimed at Chinese miners

1852 More than 20,000 Chinese people arrive in San Francisco to head to the goldfields

May 1863 Alder Gulch, Montana, gold rush starts

1857 Gold discovered in Fraser Canyon, British Columbia

1874 Gold discovered on Lakota tribal lands in the Black Hills of South Dakota

December 23, 1863 Montana Vigilantes form to protect miners and recover stolen property

August 16, 1896 George and Kate Carmack, Skookum Jim, and Dawson Charlie find gold in Rabbit Creek, Yukon Territory, Canada

1896

September 24, 1896 First claim on Bonanza Creek (Rabbit Creek) is registered to Jim Tagish

September 30, 1896 All of Bonanza Creek is staked

July 17, 1897 Ship *Portland* arrives in San Francisco, greeted by about 5,000 people. The Klondike Gold Rush is on.

October 1897 The book *Klondike: A Manual for Goldseekers* is published

1903 Jack London's *The Call of the Wild* is published, spreading stories of gold rushes.

1896

1906

July 14, 1897 Ship *Excelsior* lands in San Francisco with about half a million dollars of Klondike gold

Summer 1897 Ships with first prospectors arrive in Dyea and Skagway, Alaska, and Dawson City, Yukon

Summer 1899 Gold is discovered in Nome, Alaska. The Klondike Gold Rush is officially over.

1906 Jack London's *White Fang* is published

North America gold rushes. Inset maps for western USA and Alaska and British Columbia

BIBLIOGRAPHY

QUOTATIONS

Page 4: Dalberg-Acton, John. *Lectures on Modern History.* 1895.
Page 8: Hume, David. *An Enquiry Concerning Human Understanding.* chapter 10.4, 1748.
Page 16: Moore, John. *Quotations for Martial Artists.* Page 87, 2003.
Page 20: Richard Robert, Madden. *The Literary Life and Correspondence of the Countess of Blessington.* Cambridge University Press, 2012.
Page 34: Lynch, Peter. *One up on Wall Street.* Simon & Schuster, 2000.
Page 38: Jakes, John. *California Gold.* Open Road Media, 2012.

EXCERPTS

Page 6: Letter from John Walker to his parents, December 24, 1850 http://to.pbs.org/2x1Qn92
Page 10: The Virtual Museum of the City of San Francisco. The diary of John Sutter, 1854. http://www.sfmuseum.net/hist2/gold2.html
Page 14: Poetry Foundation. http://bit.ly/2uZ3LJF
Page 19: *The Shirley Letters from California Mines, 1851–1852.* Ed. By Thomas C. Russell, 1922.
Page 22: Avery, Isaac T. Letter to William B. Lenoir, Lenoir Family Papers, Southern Historical Collection, University of North Carolina at Chapel Hill.
Page 23: *California Herald,* December 26, 1848. Folio AN33 N5 C128, Beinecke Library, Yale University
Page 26: Colonial Dispatches of Vancouver Island and British Columbia. http://bit.ly/2fKYcMJ
Page 28: Christopherson, Edmund. *This Here is Montana.* Pages 58–59.
Page 32: Letter from Stanley Pearce in *Call of the Klondike,* David Meissner and Kim Richardson, Calkins Creek, 2013.
Page 36: Letter from Hiram Pierce to his wife Sara Jane, 1849. http://www.glittering.com/letters/pierce.html
Page 40: Sheriff, Bill. *Financial Post* interview. http://bit.ly/2vJ9yoo

TO FIND OUT MORE

Historical Fiction:
Greenwood, Barbara. *Gold Rush Fever: A Story of the Klondike.* Kids Can Press, 2001.

Gregory, Kristiana. *Seeds of Hope: The Gold Rush Diary of Susanna Fairchild.* Scholastic, 2003

London, Jack. *The Call of the Wild.* Dover Publications, 2013. (First published 1903.)

Waldorf, Mary. *The Gold Rush Kid.* Clarion Books, 2008.

Yep, Laurence. *Staking a Claim: The Journal of Wong Ming-Chung, a Chinese Miner.* Scholastic 2013.

Nonfiction:
Dyan, Penelope. *Gold Rush! A Kid's Guide to Techatticup Gold Mine, Eldorado Canyon, Nevada.* Bellissima Publishing, 2010.

Lourie, Peter. *Jack London and the Klondike Gold Rush.* Henry Holt and Co., 2017.

Meissner, David and Kim Richardson. *Call of the Klondike: A True Gold Rush Adventure.* Calkins Creek, 2013.

Ridge, John. *The Life and Adventures of Joaquin Murieta.* University of Oklahoma Press, 1977.

Schanzer, Rosalyn. *Gold Fever!: Tales from the California Gold Rush.* National Geographic Children's Books, 2007.

INTERNET GUIDELINES

Finding good source material on the Internet can sometimes be a challenge. When analyzing how reliable the information is, consider these points:

- Who is the author of the page? Is it an expert in the field or a person who experienced the event?
- Is the site well known and up to date? A page that has not been updated for several years probably has out-of-date information.
- Can you verify the facts with another site? Always double-check information.

- Have you checked all possible sites? Don't just look on the first page a search engine provides. Remember to try government sites and research papers.
- Have you recorded website addresses and names? Keep this data so you can backtrack and verify the information you want to use.

WEBSITES:

Ducksters Education Site
Learn interesting facts about the California Gold Rush from Ducksters:
http://www.ducksters.com/history/westward_expansion/california_gold_rush.php

Original Miners' Handbook
Read an online version of *Klondike: A Manual for Gold Seekers* published originally in 1897:
https://archive.org/stream/klondikemanualfo01bram#page/n9/mode/2up

Canadian Museum of Immigration
See some amazing primary-source photographs from the Canadian Museum of Immigration at Pier 21 website:
http://bit.ly/2zPgpyp

Sutter's Fort State Historical Park
http://www.parks.ca.gov/?page_id=485

The Perilous Journey North
University of Washington's Klondike Gold Rush collection:
http://www.lib.washington.edu/specialcollections/collections/exhibits/klondike

The History Channel
Videos and historic photographs to give a short history of the Yukon Gold Rush:
http://bit.ly/2z6UBRB

Klondike Gold Rush National Historic Park
https://www.nps.gov/klgo/index.htm

Bodie State Historic Park
https://www.bodie.com/

Kids Encyclopedia
Check out more images, newspaper articles, and maps of the Klondike Gold Rush from Kiddle:
https://kids.kiddle.co/Klondike_Gold_Rush

GLOSSARY

archives Places to store collections of records

artifacts Objects made by humans

auditory Related to hearing

bias Prejudice in favor of or against one thing, person, or group. Primary and secondary sources of evidence may show bias.

bonanza A boom, or sudden win or rush of success

boomtown A town that grows quickly as people flood in to work, live, and set up businesses

colony A region governed by another country; a group of people from the same background living together

con man A person that gains trust to trick people out of money; short for "confidence man"

conservators People who repair and protect artifacts

context Things that influence and are happening during an event that help historical understanding

cremation Burning of a dead body

critically Analyzing the good and bad of a subject

culture The ideas, customs, and behaviors of a distinct people

deposit A layer of a metal left in soil or rocks by nature

disrupted Changed greatly or destroyed

diverted Changed the course of a river

documents Written or printed materials such as claims forms, reports, and treaties

encroached Intruded on someone else's territory or rights

evidence A collection of facts or information to show whether something is true. Primary and secondary sources are used as evidence.

expansion The process of growing larger

famine Severe food shortage

Forty-niners People who traveled to California to find gold in the rush of 1849 to 1852

ghost towns Towns abandoned by people as work dries up

gulch A very narrow canyon

historian A person who studies evidence from or about a particular time or event that has happened in the past

human rights abuses Acts withholding such needs of people as food, homes, freedom, and good wages

hydraulic Using water pressure to remove gold-bearing dirt from the sides of hills or mountains

immigration People coming into a country to live from another country

Indigenous peoples People who live in a place before first contact by explorers; includes American Indians (also known as Native Americans) and First Nation Peoples

inflow A large amount of people coming into an area

interpretation The analysis and explanation of the meaning of evidence

isolated Far away from other places

land recorder's office Office to which miners went to stake their claim to mine

land treaties Agreements between Indigenous peoples and foreign governments for use of land

merchant A person who buys and sells goods

militia A military force made of ordinary people

mine tailings Leftover soil and rocks when gold is removed

minerals Natural solid substances

mint A place where coins are made

moccasins A soft leather shoe made and worn by some Indigenous peoples of North America

natural resources Materials in nature that can be used in business or industry

ore Rock from which minerals are extracted

paper trail A series of reports

pay streak A layer of soil and rock containing metal

permanent Lasting forever

perspective Point of view

portraying Showing or representing something

prejudice An opinion for or against something

preserved Kept in good condition

primary sources Firsthand memories, accounts, documents, or artifacts from the past that serve as historical records about what happened at a particular time or event

quartz A mineral rich in silicon, the basis of sand

quick and dirty An inexpensive diner, sometimes called a "greasy spoon"

remote Far away and often hard to reach

reserves A supply left behind

river steamer A riverboat that runs on steam

saloon A place where alcoholic drinks are sold

sculpted Something made by carving or shaping

secondary sources Evidence of an event usually created some time after it happened; a historian's or artist's interpretations of primary sources

settlement A place where people live: a mining camp, town, or city; people making homes in an area

sluices Artificial channels of water used to separate gold from soil and rocks

society A group of people forming a single community with its own distinctive culture and institutions

source materials Collections of historical evidence

stake To get the rights to mine a piece of land by putting posts in the ground

status Someone's position in society

telegraphy Sending messages long distance in coded form as electrical signals along wires

tertiary Third in order

tramways Boxes, or cars, on rails pulled by cables

tributary A small stream that flows into a bigger river or lake

uncharted Not surveyed and located on a map

vigilante Ordinary people who act as law officers

visual Referring to images you can see

waterway A route for water, made by nature or humans

INDEX